SWITZERLAND

EXPLORE THE COUNTRIES · EXPLORE THE COUNTRIES · EXPLORE THE COUNTRIES · EXPLORE THE COUNTRIES

Big Buddy Books
An Imprint of Abdo Publishing
abdopublishing.com

Julie Murray

abdopublishing.com

Published by Abdo Publishing, a division of ABDO, PO Box 398166, Minneapolis, Minnesota 55439.
Copyright © 2016 by Abdo Consulting Group, Inc. International copyrights reserved in all countries. No part
of this book may be reproduced in any form without written permission from the publisher. Big Buddy Books™
is a trademark and logo of Abdo Publishing.

Printed in the United States of America, North Mankato, Minnesota.
092015
012016

THIS BOOK CONTAINS
RECYCLED MATERIALS

Cover Photo: Shutterstock.com.
Interior Photos: ARCO/Marschall, H./Glow Images (p. 16); Buyenlarge/Getty Images (p. 17); © Corbis (p. 31);
    David Hanson/Getty Images (p. 19); Hoberman Collection/Getty Images (p. 25); © imageBROKER/Alamy
    (p. 34); © iStockphoto.com (p. 15); Christian Kober/Getty Images (p. 35); JONATHAN NACKSTRAND/
    Getty Images (p. 29); Print Collector/Getty Images (p. 33); Science & Society Picture Library/Getty
    Images (p. 13); Shutterstock.com (pp. 5, 9, 11, 13, 19, 21, 23, 27, 33, 34, 35, 37, 38).

Coordinating Series Editor: Megan M. Gunderson
Editor: Katie Lajiness
Contributing Editors: Bridget O'Brien, Marcia Zappa
Graphic Design: Adam Craven

Country population and area figures taken from the CIA World Factbook.

Library of Congress Cataloging-in-Publication Data

Murray, Julie, 1969-
 Switzerland / Julie Murray.
    pages cm. -- (Explore the countries)
 Includes index.
 ISBN 978-1-68078-071-0
1. Switzerland--Juvenile literature. I. Title.
DQ17.M88 2015
949.4--dc23
                            2015022672

SWITZERLAND

CONTENTS

AROUND THE WORLD

Our world has many countries. Each country has beautiful land. It has its own rich history. And, the people have their own languages and ways of life.

Switzerland is a country in Europe. What do you know about Switzerland? Let's learn more about this place and its story!

Did You Know?

Switzerland is almost twice the size of New Jersey.

The Swiss Alps are a mountain range in southern and eastern Switzerland. They cover more than half of the country.

PASSPORT TO SWITZERLAND

Switzerland shares its borders with five countries. France is to the west and Germany is to the north. Liechtenstein and Austria are to the east. Italy is to the south.

Switzerland's total area is 15,937 square miles (41,277 sq km). More than 8.1 million people live in Switzerland.

Did You Know?

People from Switzerland are called Swiss.

WHERE IN THE WORLD?

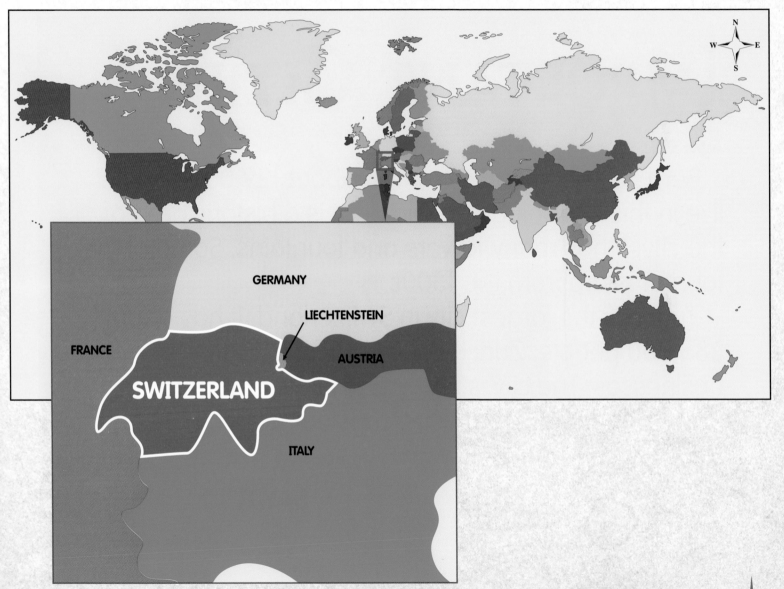

GERMANY

LIECHTENSTEIN

FRANCE

AUSTRIA

SWITZERLAND

ITALY

IMPORTANT CITIES

Bern is Switzerland's **capital**. About 129,000 people live in this charming city. Old Bern is a historic area of the city. It has many towers and fountains. Some of the fountains are from the 1500s.

Zurich is the largest city in Switzerland. It has about 385,000 people. Zurich is famous for its banking businesses. The city is known for its large areas of grass and trees. A park stretches out to the shores of Lake Zurich.

SAY IT
Bern
BUHRN
Zurich
ZUR-ihk

8

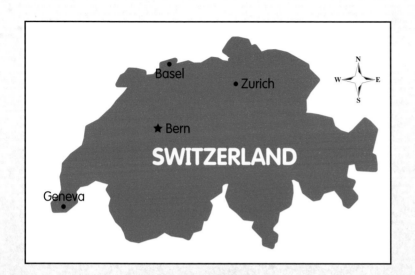

Zurich's Saint Peter church has the largest clockface in Europe.

Emmentaler cheese was created near Bern. In the United States, it is known as Swiss cheese.

Geneva is the second-largest city in Switzerland. It has more than 192,000 people. The European headquarters for the United Nations (UN) is in Geneva. The UN helps keep the peace around the world. Switzerland joined this organization in 2002.

Basel is the third-largest city in Switzerland. About 167,000 people live there. Basel is home to the oldest university in Switzerland. The school dates back to 1460.

SAY IT

Geneva
juh-NEE-vuh

Basel
BA-zil

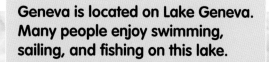
Geneva is located on Lake Geneva. Many people enjoy swimming, sailing, and fishing on this lake.

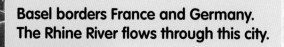
Basel borders France and Germany. The Rhine River flows through this city.

Switzerland in History

SAY IT

Canton
CAN-tan

Around 800 BC, **Celts** built settlements in the area that is now Switzerland. They lived on single farms or in villages. The Celts were known for their beautiful gold jewelry.

Beginning in 1291, the Swiss Confederation formed when three cantons came together. They guarded themselves against attackers.

Many important Swiss banks opened in the 1700s. A bank could not share information about whose money it held. Today, Swiss banks are still famous for being secretive.

Alpenhorns were first used nearly 2,000 years ago in the northern Alps. Celtic tribes used alpenhorns to call to villagers across mountain valleys.

Swiss banks grew by helping rich merchants manage their money.

People were very hungry from 1816 to 1817. There was not enough food because of many nearby wars. But soon, farming improved.

During the 1900s, almost all the countries in Europe fought in **World War I** and **World War II**. Switzerland did not fight or take sides. Switzerland is now a powerful and peaceful country.

Today, people from around the world visit Switzerland for fun. This is important to the country's success. Rhine Falls in northern Switzerland is one popular place to visit. It is the largest waterfall in Europe.

TIMELINE

1815

Switzerland decided to not fight or take sides in any war. This decision still stands today.

1020

The Castle of Habsburg was built near present-day Aarau. A royal German family controlled the area and lived in this castle.

1291

The leaders of three Swiss cantons signed the Perpetual Covenant. This agreement was the start of the Swiss Confederation.

1880-1881

Swiss writer Johanna Spyri printed the classic children's book *Heidi* in two books. The character Heidi lives in the Swiss mountains. Her parents are not alive, so she lives with her grandfather.

1971

Women won the right to vote and take part in **federal** elections.

2015

The remains of an ancient animal called a woolly mammoth were discovered in central Switzerland. These animals had lots of hair and long, curved teeth called tusks. Scientists believe the remains are around 20,000 years old.

An Important Symbol

Switzerland's flag is a white cross on a red background. The cross represents **Christianity**. The flag was legally established in the late 1800s.

Switzerland's government is a confederation. A confederation is an agreement between multiple areas to work with each other.

Switzerland is divided into 26 cantons. A canton is similar to a state. Each of these small territories has its own government and courts.

The Swiss first used a white cross on their flag back in the 1300s!

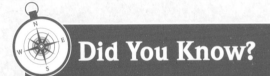

Did You Know?

Switzerland is one of only two nations with a square flag. Most countries have rectangle flags.

Each Swiss canton has one or more official languages. The official languages in most of the cantons are French, German, or Italian.

19

ACROSS THE LAND

The weather patterns in Switzerland are different throughout the country. Switzerland's **plateau** is warm during the summer, often with fog and rain. Snow is common on the plateau during both mild and cold winters. The highest areas in the Swiss Alps have snow all year.

Glaciers helped form the Swiss Alps. These mountains are part of a larger mountain range called the Alps. The Alps are the biggest mountain system in Europe. They are a popular place to go skiing.

The Swiss plateau is between the Jura Mountains and the Alps. It has many hills and lakes.

Many types of animals make their home in Switzerland. Alpine marmots live in high meadows. They are small animals with large front teeth. Ibex live in the Swiss mountains. These wild goats have curved horns, and they eat grass.

Different plants grow in Switzerland, depending on the area. Beech and oak trees grow in the west. Spruce trees grow in the north.

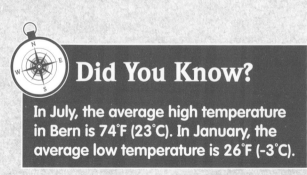

Did You Know?

In July, the average high temperature in Bern is 74°F (23°C). In January, the average low temperature is 26°F (-3°C).

Saint Bernard dogs were bred and trained to rescue people in the Alps.

Many people visit the Alps for the fresh air and great views.

23

EARNING A LIVING

All men in Switzerland must serve in the military between the ages of 19 and 26. Women can serve in the military, too. The military helps keep the peace around the world. But, Switzerland does not fight in wars.

Many Swiss work in banking or help create goods. The Swiss are known for making excellent watches and Swiss Army knives. They also make foods such as chocolate and cheese.

Switzerland has small amounts of iron and manganese in the ground. People mine lime, salt, sand, gravel, clay, and marble.

Did You Know?

Swiss Army knives are more than just knives! They are known for including can openers, screwdrivers, scissors, and other tools all in one handy device.

Many types of cheeses are made in Switzerland. This includes Appenzeller, Spalen, and Gomser.

LIFE IN SWITZERLAND

There are many old churches in Switzerland. Many people are **Christian**. A small population is **Muslim** or **Jewish**.

People from around the world like shopping in Zurich. Stores there sell fancy jewelry and watches. They also sell books and crafts. Crafts include fine wood pieces such as spoons and stools.

Switzerland has many tasty foods. Rösti is made of cooked potatoes. Bratwurst is a kind of sausage. These foods are often paired together.

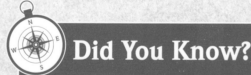

Did You Know?

In Switzerland, children must attend school from ages 7 to 16. The average person receives 16 years of education.

Zurich's Bahnhofstrasse is a street with many stores. People can buy watches, clothing, and more.

SAY IT

Bahnhofstrasse
bahn-hahf-STRASS

Music, poems, and dancing are all Swiss folk arts. Many songs are about the history of Switzerland.

Yodeling is a **traditional** type of singing in mountain areas of Switzerland. It includes many changes from an ordinary singing voice to a high voice. Herders may yodel to call their livestock.

Winter sports are very popular in Switzerland. Many people enjoy skiing and ice hockey.

Did You Know?

Switzerland hosted the Winter Olympics in 1928 and 1948.

In 2015, Switzerland played at the Ice Hockey World Championship. They lost to the United States in the first round.

FAMOUS FACES

Many smart Swiss people helped change the world with their great ideas. Carl Jung was born on July 26, 1875, in Kesswil, Switzerland. He formed many **theories** about the mind and dreams. Jung's ideas shaped the way we think about how people act! He died on June 6, 1961.

SAY IT
Jung *YUNG*

Carl Jung taught at the Federal Polytechnical University in Zurich. His ideas are still taught in schools today.

Albert Einstein was a famous scientist. He was born on March 14, 1879 in Ulm, Germany. Einstein went to school in Switzerland. He was a Swiss citizen from 1901 to 1914. Einstein had advanced ideas about time, space, matter, and other areas of science. He died on April 18, 1955.

Roger Federer was born on August 8, 1981. He won his 1,000th tennis match in 2015. He was ranked one of the best tennis players in the world.

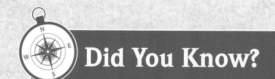

Did You Know?

Einstein won the Nobel Prize for physics in 1921. These prizes are awarded in six areas for outstanding accomplishments.

Einstein attended the Federal Institute of Technology in Zurich from 1896 to 1900. He studied math and physics, the science of matter and motion.

Roger Federer has won more Grand Slam singles events than any other male. These are the most important tennis events.

TOUR BOOK

Imagine traveling to Switzerland! Here are some places you could go and things you could do.

 ## Explore

Lake Geneva is one of the largest lakes in Europe. It is between France and Switzerland. People enjoy ferryboat rides on this beautiful lake.

 ## Celebrate

Swiss National Day is August 1. The holiday honors the forming of Switzerland. The Rhine Falls waterfall is lit up for the day.

 # Eat

Fondue is a Swiss meal of melted cheese served in a shared pot. People use long forks to dip pieces of bread in the pot.

 # See

Visit the Swiss National Museum in Zurich. See important objects from Switzerland's history.

 # Play

Many places in Switzerland honor the holiday Fasnacht, or carnival. In Basel, there is a three-day event. The city's streetlights are turned off so that the only light comes from lanterns. People in masks and costumes put on parades.

A Great Country

   The story of Switzerland is important to our world. Switzerland is a land with soaring mountains and a rich history. It is a country of peace and wealth.

   The people and places that make up Switzerland offer something special. They help make the world a more beautiful, interesting place.

The Chillon Castle sits on the shore of Lake Geneva. The castle is the most-visited historical building in Switzerland.

SWITZERLAND UP CLOSE

Official Name: Swiss Confederation

Flag:

Population (rank): 8,121,830
(July 2015 est.)
(96th most-populated country)

Total Area (rank): 15,937 square miles
(136th largest country)

Capital: Bern

Official Languages: German, French, Italian, Romansch

Currency: Swiss franc

Form of Government: Confederation

National Anthem: "Swiss Psalm"

IMPORTANT WORDS

capital a city where government leaders meet.

Celts (KEHLTS) people who lived about 2,000 years ago in many countries of western Europe.

Christian (KRIHS-chuhn) a person who practices Christianity, which is a religion that follows the teachings of Jesus Christ.

federal of or relating to the central government.

glacier (GLAY-shuhr) a huge chunk of ice and snow on land.

Jewish a person who practices Judaism, which is a religion based on laws recorded in the Torah, or is related to the ancient Hebrews.

Muslim a person who practices Islam, which is a religion based on a belief in Allah as God and Muhammad as his prophet.

plateau (pla-TOH) a raised area of flat land.

theory an explanation of how or why something happens.

traditional (truh-DIHSH-nuhl) relating to a tradition, which is a belief, a custom, or a story handed down from older people to younger people.

World War I a war fought in Europe from 1914 to 1918.

World War II a war fought in Europe, Asia, and Africa from 1939 to 1945.

WEBSITES

To learn more about Explore the Countries, visit **booklinks.abdopublishing.com**. These links are routinely monitored and updated to provide the most current information available.

INDEX